DSC SPEED READS
COMMUNICATIONS

Report Writing

Janet Owens

DIRECTORY OF SOCIAL CHANGE

Published by
Directory of Social Change
24 Stephenson Way
London NW1 2DP
Tel. 08450 77 77 07; Fax 020 7391 4804
email publications@dsc.org.uk
www.dsc.org.uk
from whom further copies and a full books catalogue are available.

Directory of Social Change is a Registered Charity no. 800517

First published 2011

Copyright © Directory of Social Change 2011

The moral right of the authors has been asserted in accordance with the Copyright, Designs and Patents Act 1988.

All rights reserved. **No part of this book may be stored in a retrieval system or reproduced in any form whatsoever without prior permission in writing from the publisher.**
This book is sold subject to the condition that it shall not, by way of trade or otherwise, be lent, re-sold, hired out or otherwise circulated without the publisher's prior permission in any form of binding or cover other than that in which it is published, and without a similar condition including this condition being imposed on the subsequent purchaser.

ISBN 978 1 906294 16 8

British Library Cataloguing in Publication Data

A catalogue record for this book is available from the British Library

Cover and text designed by Kate Bass
Typeset by Marlinzo Services, Frome
Printed and bound by Martins the Printers, Berwick-upon-Tweed

All Directory of Social Change departments in London:
08450 77 77 07

Directory of Social Change Northern Office:
Research 0151 708 0136

For other titles in the DSC SPEED READ series go to:
www.dsc.org.uk/Publications/SpeedReadSeries

Contents

Introduction	4
Chapter 1: What is a report?	**5**
▪ Types of report	5
▪ The character of your report	6
▪ Structure and elements of a report	7
▪ The formalities	9
Chapter 2: Purpose and audience	**13**
▪ The commissioner	13
▪ Why reports fail	13
▪ The themes of a report	14
▪ Varied readership	15
▪ Single readership	15
Chapter 3: Planning	**16**
▪ Activity	16
▪ Procrastination	17
▪ Collection, organisation and collation	19
Chapter 4: Appropriate language	**22**
▪ Good English	22
▪ Readability tools	23
▪ Presenting your organisation	23
Chapter 5: The writing process	**25**
▪ Writing stages	25
▪ Rewards	32
▪ Continuous improvement	32

Introduction

Who will this book help?

This practical guide will help those who would like to take some of the anxiety out of writing. It is a guide for people who have not had training or much experience of formal business writing and a quick easy reference guide for those who have. It will be useful for people whose time is at a premium.

What will it give you?

This book will give you practical tools and guidance on how to write short, medium and longer reports in the context of day-to-day management. It adopts a systematic approach to report writing and will help you from the planning stage to writing and revision. It can be easily adapted to suit a variety of needs and will also provide transferable skills which are useful in any aspect of working life.

Chapter 1

What is a report?

This chapter explains what a report is, how to characterise it and the key structural elements of which you should be aware.

Types of report

A report can mean different things to different people. Begin by thinking about the kind of reports you write and for whom. Reports are formal documents that present information tailored to a given situation and audience, and can fall into a number of different categories.

They may be:

- giving facts
- reporting details
- explaining or informing
- motivating and leading readers to make decisions.

There are many other reasons why a report may be required. The point is that you, as the writer, need to know the reason for your report.

The character of your report

A report can be many a varied thing, and defining its nature is one of the first challenges. Here are some good questions to ask at the beginning of the process.

What am I really trying to do?
What is the purpose of the report?
Who is the audience?

However, these questions are not simply useful at the initiation stage of the report, but can be asked throughout the whole writing process. Putting these kinds of question to yourself is one of the keys to success: it keeps you focused and prevents the material from becoming too divergent or detailed.

Categorising your report

Having established the need, purpose and audience, you can decide the category of your report.

- If it is in response to a request for information, perhaps from a funder, then usually the character and format is already decided by them and you will respond accordingly.
- If facts are being presented, you will be informing the reader by a straightforward presentation of those facts. Make them stand out from any background material.
- If the report is a leading report, it will be trying to motivate its reader. This calls for persuasive analysis and well-presented arguments that build to a clear conclusion.
- If you are trying to instruct your reader, then clear explanations are required. Direct instruction rather than persuasion will take a more decisive format.

> **Top tip**
>
> Think of a report that you remember reading. Why do you remember it? If it was good, why was that? If it was bad, what irritated you? Think about how your report will be received.

Size

What dictates the length of a report? A report should be as concise as possible while still clearly conveying the necessary information. Often, the length as well as the nature of the report dictates the structure of how the message is conveyed. Small reports are usually considered to be those containing up to about 2,000 words. Medium-sized reports run to 2,000 to 5,000 words, and long reports are more than 5,000 words. The size of the report usually dictates how the work should be divided up.

Structure and elements of a report

A research report contains headings and sections which can be useful for all reports. The master template that follows can be adapted in different ways according to the nature of the report. Long reports can use the template in full.

The template

A report will usually consist of all or some of the following sections.

Title page

This is the first page of a large report, often with the title and a brief qualifier of the nature of the subject: for example, 'Fitting the Pieces Together: An Action Learning Set for Staff'. It will also usually state the author's name, which may be one or more people, a department or the organisation.

Medium-sized and short reports may have no title page but simply a heading at the top of the first page. The organisational logo, author's name and contact details are also often shown in reports of these sizes.

> **Where next?**
> DSC runs a course on effective report writing. To find out more go to: www.dsc.org.uk/reportwriting

Top tip

The AutoSummarize function in Microsoft Word is a really handy tool that can save you time by creating a good starting point for your summary. It can also indicate the quality of the report's structure: if the auto-summary isn't very accurate your report's structure might need to be improved.

Ben Wittenberg, Director of Publishing, Policy and Research, DSC

Where next?

To learn how to AutoSummarize a document, go to: www.microsoft.com/education/autosummarize.aspx

Summary

This is a brief synopsis *of all* of the content of the report. In technical papers this is called an abstract. The summary is an invitation to read the rest of the report and, although it is placed at the beginning, it is usually written after everything else is complete. Be aware that the summary may be all that is read by some of your intended audience, such as your chief executive, and so it is important that it captures the key information.

For medium-sized reports this becomes a simple summary, and for short reports it can be a sentence or two providing an overview of the subject.

Introduction

This provides a broad outline of the purpose of the document. The aims are stated and put into context. Medium-sized reports also need a brief statement of intent. Shorter ones usually do not need this section.

Objectives and methods

What is going to be explored and recorded and how this is going to be done is the work of this section. Full details should be given here, as well as diagrams or graphs if they are being used. Medium-sized reports will section this as 'procedure', and short reports as 'task identification', with brief notes supplied accordingly.

Findings or results

This section records all the facts and findings in a logical, clear sequence.

For medium-sized and short reports this section, when read with the conclusions, is likely to suffice.

Conclusion

The conclusion is an interpretation of the facts. It informs the reader where you hope they will go next. It may lead them to actions or suggest how they can use the information.

In medium-sized and short reports, conclusions may be combined with recommendations. They may make a number of suggestions, drawing out the knowledge that has been imparted in the findings or results section, and indicate how this may be used by the reader.

Recommendations

Recommendations are distinct from conclusions. They may contain a call to action or for further work to be carried out. They may also come at the front and be the first section that some people will read. However, they are not the same as the summary, which is a synopsis of the whole report.

References

A list is required of all the references made to other pieces of work. This is not usually necessary for shorter reports.

Appendices

Add to the report any material that you think might be helpful to the reader. However, do not overload this final section. The previous headings should have covered most of the information you wish to give them. Only additional, really necessary, documentation should be attached here.

Medium-sized reports may like to have this section and fill it with small amounts of additional detail, such as a financial page if the report did not have that subject as its main topic. Short reports do not normally require an appendix.

The formalities

One important thing to remember is that the headings outlined in this chapter are indications of the sections of a formal report. In most reports these sections may

> **Top tip**
>
> For highly referenced reports it is essential that you make full notes on reference material during your research phase. You will tear your hair out if you try to find them all at the end of the process.
>
> John Martin, Publisher, DSC

be named less formally. For example, the summary might read 'Why this report?', the introduction could be 'The main priorities', or the findings and discussion paragraphs called 'The debate'. The idea is that a tried and tested format is applied, in order to ensure that readers can progress through the report in a clear and signposted manner.

The following excerpts are from a report written as a result of a board review of Crossroads and are used with their kind permission. Note the use of relevant parts of the framework. There was an additional section: Recommendations. The full report was 2,000 words.

Case study

**CROSSROADS CARING FOR CARERS
(SALFORD, TRAFFORD AND STOCKPORT)
Board review**

Why a review?

The board of trustees recognised that it should set aside time to reflect on its own performance and functioning as a board.

The key principles

The skills of the board were to be audited in the self assessment of skills (appendix 1).
This to be followed by an individual discussion questionnaire (appendix 2) to ascertain the future direction of the organisation.
These actions to be taken with the awareness that the board should have a strategy for its own effectiveness in order to take the necessary steps to ensure the continuation of the excellent work of Crossroads.

...continued

Board members

[All the board members took part. The names of the members were listed here.]

The review

Conducted in accordance with the relevant sections in the NCVO's document 'Good Governance' (www.ncvo-vol.org.uk and follow the links).

Confidentiality was maintained if requested, but otherwise all information provided was to be used as part of the material for the review.

An external resource was used to process the audit, facilitate the discussion meetings and write the report.

The board members' self assessment of skills

All the members completed an emailed audit. The questions addressed were:
Contribution to the board
Main skills/expertise
Commitment
List of skills

Findings

Contributions were offered in these areas: caring; finance; local authority; networking; policies; administration; small business management; NHS systems; resource and strategy planning and private industry.

Main skills and expertise noted were: caring experience; board experience; financial; change management and its processes; performance management; service development; knowledge of health and social care fields and counselling.

Commitment was recognised from both long-term and new members of the Crossroads board. There was a strong desire to see the organisation thrive in the current climate where new development ideas will be required. An attitude of pride and loyalty prevailed together with an admiration of the work done by Crossroads.

...continued

List of skills
[The results were recorded here.]

Conclusions
Audit narratives and lists of skills suggest that the board has members with the diverse range of background knowledge, skills and expertise required to run the organisation effectively.

In order to respond to the challenges and opportunities in the future, however, attention needs to be drawn to the small number of people responding to the areas of legal and marketing skills in particular, and also the areas of property management and information technology. A balanced board would also consider its diversity of membership.

Recommendations
Recruitment of new board members with the appropriate skills is necessary. The NCVO offers a free service advertising vacancies.

Induction training should be offered for all new members. This is to ensure that they can carry out their new role proficiently.

Specific and wise use of the existing skill bank will enhance the board's efficiency. This may be done by allowing members to be responsible for particular areas of work either within the main board or on subcommittees.

Training in certain areas could be offered to individuals who wish to increase their knowledge in a directional manner, which would bring a particular element of use to the committee.

Co-options may be considered. The two local authorities not represented on the current board could be approached.

All board members should receive the necessary training and ongoing support needed to discharge their duties.

Appendix 1
Board members' self assessment of skills

Appendix 2
Individual discussion questionnaire

Chapter 2

Purpose and audience

Reports are written for a variety of audiences. This chapter shows how understanding your audience will help to inform your purpose.

The commissioner

If your report has been commissioned, the onus is on the person or people responsible to brief you by communicating their requirements: their vision of the end product. Perhaps it is your boss, a board of trustees or an external source requiring information. You need to be clear who that agent is, and what they are hoping for at the end of the process.

If the idea for the report is your own, it is up to you to be clear in your own mind why the report is needed.

Why reports fail

One of the most common reasons why a report fails is omitting to identify why you are writing and who you are writing for: in other words, its purpose was unclear at the beginning. The result is that too many issues are gathered together and become entangled, so the reader is left with an indecisive or inconclusive report, and they may never finish reading the report at all. A confused writer will always produce a confused reader.

Doing all of the following things should give you a definite framework to be clear about the purpose of your writing and how you may proceed.

Checklist
- Be clear exactly who is commissioning the writing.
- Who is the intended readership or audience for the report?
- Know the limit of your authority – this means knowing precisely what you can and can't write, and where your level of authority to make any kind of statement begins and ends.
- Understand the availability and access that you may need to other people, internal and external data and their copyright status.
- Check the confidentiality policy of your organisation – check how this affects your writing.
- Be aware of the budget that you have been granted, if any. At the same time, confirm all the other resources that you may need, such as members of staff and their time.

> **Top tip**
> Try writing your purpose in one or two concise sentences. For complex documents with a number of individual elements, write one sentence for each purpose.

The themes of a report

Some reports have single themes. A funder may simply wish to have a narrative to support the figures already supplied in a financial report. If there is to be only one type of readership, then the purpose is clear. Providing the facts with details given as case studies or stories is usually what is required.

However, most reports have either a varied readership or one particular body of readers who are expecting several issues to be covered in the one report.

Varied readership

Try to guess what the reactions of each of the groups of readers might be. Every potential group will have their own individual concerns or agenda. Attempt to 'get alongside' them and write with this in mind. Know what their potential reactions might be. Are you expecting commitment to your ideas or opposition? Be aware of this, and address these anticipated reactions.

Single readership

The purpose of many reports is to provide information for a group of people that need to know the current situation, and are looking to move things forward on the basis of the report. Often, boards of trustees are recipients of such material (see p. 10 for a case study that outlines a board review report).

Top tip

If you have access to other reports written for the same audience you can quickly get a feel for the appropriate style and level for your report.

John Martin, Publisher, DSC

Chapter 3

Planning

Planning your report is crucial. In this chapter, we look at the processes involved and the blockages to getting started.

Are you the kind of person who leaps into action at every opportunity? Or are you perhaps a reflector who prefers to take time over every decision and action? Reflection is good, but procrastination is not. Similarly, activity is good, but jumping in with both feet is not. When setting out to write a report, both reflection and activity are needed.

Activity

Top tip

Before you decide how to write the report, plan what you will write about and know why you are writing.

Activity is certainly necessary in the initial stage of report writing. Consider Rudyard Kipling's famous quote from 'The Elephant's Child' (*Just So Stories*, 1902):

*I keep six honest serving-men
(They taught me all I knew);
Their names are What and Why and When
And How and Where and Who.*

- What are you writing about?
- Why are you writing at all?
- Where will you write and where will you be presenting the material?
- When will you be required to finish, and when will you aim to complete each stage of the writing?
- Who is your audience?
- How will you present your work?

A certain degree of industriousness is required in gathering the material before you begin to compile the report.

Exercise

Do a mental check and note down the sources of your material. The obvious may be statistics, service results or records of meetings. However, remember that all your material has been collating in your brain and other external sources will have impacted on this. So, add other literature which may have influenced your data gathering.

Procrastination

It is probably safe to say that all of us procrastinate from time to time. However, knowing why we procrastinate can help to prevent it. Here are some of the main reasons why we put off until tomorrow what we should be doing today, and how you can avoid them.

> Where next?
> *Achieve*, M Butcher, DSC, 2003.

Feeling overwhelmed

When preparing to write a report, it may seem like there is too much material or even too little. The task becomes enormous. The answer is, of course, to break it down into small pieces. We have all heard this many times and it is often easier said than done. It is especially difficult when it is the lack of material that is overwhelming. Yet breaking things into chunks is still the answer.

Put all the bits you have out in front of you in any format you like. Next, get all the pieces of information that link together in any way and put them to one side. Keep doing this until you can see the patterns or gaps. You may also find some overlaps. Discard the extraneous (but not permanently, in case you change your mind). Mind maps can help you to break up your thoughts and to generate more ideas, if that is what you need.

Mind maps

Mind maps are 'brain friendly'. The brain stores information by association in clusters, not in linear form. This is the reason why mind maps are easy to remember. They are very like spider graphs.

A spider graph (sometimes called a semantic map) is a type of graphic organiser that is used to investigate and enumerate various aspects of a single theme or topic, helping the writer to organise their thoughts. It looks a bit like a spider's web, hence its name.

The process of creating a spider graph helps the writer focus on the topic and requires them to review what they already know in order to organise that knowledge. The process helps the writer to monitor their growing comprehension of the topic. It helps to point out the areas where the writer must investigate more in order to fill out the web.

Try drawing a mind map or spider graph by using key words, not sentences, and by enhancing the words with colours, illustrations and symbols. Then show the connections.

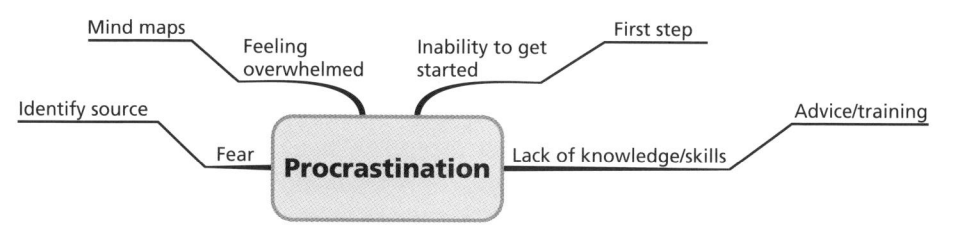

> **Where next?**
>
> *The Mind Map Book*, T Buzan and B Buzan, BBC Active, 2006.

Procrastination mind map branches:
- Mind maps
- Feeling overwhelmed
- Inability to get started
- First step
- Identify source
- Fear
- Lack of knowledge/skills
- Advice/training

Fear

This is an instinctive reaction designed to make us get as far away from the cause of the fear as possible, so we avoid the activity associated with the fear. This element of fear almost always underlies the tendency to procrastinate. It may be fear of failure (or even success), fear of not doing something well enough (perfectionists will recognise this), or fear of being exposed in some way. The best thing to do is to get to grips with the fear. When you are clearer about what the fear is, you can find a creative way to address it.

Lack of knowledge, skills or understanding

This gap can delay our start. Find out what is missing and begin to seek help, advice or training.

Inability to get started

This is the hardest thing for procrastinators. The key is to simply take the first step.

Collection, organisation and collation

Planning for these activities is important, so remember to schedule time to do all of this. You might like to draw up a timetable and section each activity with its components.

Collection

Dos and Don'ts

Do check that everything you have selected is factually accurate.

Don't mislead or misinform your readers.

Do verify all the facts you have.

Don't misinterpret facts.

Do be objective about the details and the wider picture you are going to present.

> **Where next?**
>
> These sections are influenced by ideas from 'Coaching Tip – Beating Procrastination' © Annabel Sutton, www.annabelsutton.com, 2009.

Don't be subjective or 'bend' information to suit your cause.
Do be logical in your selection.
Don't reflect your emotions.
Do use material that will produce unbiased conclusions.
Don't keep data that will reflect any prejudiced opinions.
Do store for use items that you know will be acceptable to your readers.
Don't project sources of disagreement.
Do keep an open mind for interesting pieces that will enhance the reading.
Don't bore your readers.
Do discuss possible material with your commissioning agent (if you have one).
Don't forget to include your prospective readers.
Do check that you have sufficient information to complete the task.
Don't leave too little time for all this collection.

> **Top tip**
> Construct a solid argument. Highlight findings that support your recommendations, but do not ignore other findings. Consider your purpose and your audience when selecting the evidence.

Organisation

If you know your purpose, you can communicate your message better. Significant facts will stand out from general background information. This makes it easier for readers to see your argument and recommendations.

Get your ideas down on paper: write down anything that comes to mind. Do your research and add to your notes. Make a list or a mind map: invariably, it will contain too much, so decide what to keep and what to leave out by editing down to the core considerations. Always keep in mind your purpose and the audience.

Collation

Decide on the conclusions and the recommendations (that you will make in response to any problems that the report will identify) early in the collation of material, and put them at the bottom of your plan. Design headings as signposts for the reader and lead them to your conclusions. Have a clear, logical series of steps prepared before you begin to write that will make up your sections and that the reader can follow easily. This should be kept to a brief and succinct outline. Remember your purpose and the report objectives and make sure that the outline encompasses them.

Chapter 4

Appropriate language

This chapter looks at using accessible language and readability tools, and presenting your organisation.

Good English

In everyday speech we often use accessible English instinctively. For example, we would say to a child: 'Be careful – a car is coming!', not 'Beware of an oncoming vehicle'. Yet when writing a report, somehow our preconceptions of what is expected of this kind of writing too often turns our normal sensible English into overbearing jargon and outdated formal English.

Is there such a thing as good English? Yes: it is appropriate and Plain English. It is writing in a style and at a level that suits the organisation from which it is written, as well as its readers.

When thinking about whether you are choosing the right language for your report, ask yourself these questions.

Checklist
- Will readers understand the report easily?
- Do your chosen words or phrases convey your intended meaning?

> **Where next?**
> The Plain English Campaign, www.plainenglish.co.uk

- Have you used the right words or phrases for the context?
- Are you using jargon, unexplained abbreviations or acronyms?
- Is there a more succinct expression – have you used three words when you could use one?
- Is there a more powerful and descriptive word you could have used?

The key to good report writing is being appropriate. Know your audience and the vocabulary that they are familiar with and will understand. Remember that you are writing for them, rather than for yourself. Technical language can be a shortcut to precise understanding if used correctly, but it can be gobbledygook if not.

Readability tools

The Gunning Fog Index is one of the best known linguistic tests designed to measure readability. However, it is best applied to writing that is to be read by large segments of the population, and so it is often applied to newspapers.

For your report writing you are more likely to benefit from the readability tools in word-processing programmes. Microsoft Word, for example, can display readability statistics. If the 'show readability statistics' box is checked as an option in the 'tools' menu, when you use the spelling and grammar function on the standard toolbar, it displays a comprehension rating when you have completed the spelling or grammar check.

Presenting your organisation

When you write a report, particularly if it has an external audience, be aware that you are presenting an image of your organisation. The tone and style of

> **Top tip**
>
> In the same way as weeds are described by gardeners as simply flowers in the wrong place, jargon is technical language used in the wrong place for an inappropriate audience.
>
> **John Martin, Publisher, DSC**

> **Where next?**
>
> The Microsoft Flesch-Kincaid readability test: tinyurl.com/TestReadability

Appropriate language

> **Top tip**
>
> Gather a number of newspapers, magazines, newsletters and textbooks and look at how you can tell the sources by only a quick glance. What does your audience glean about you and your organisation from a swift review of your reports?

> **Where next?**
>
> For a bit of fun, try the Plain English Campaign's wonderful Gobbledygook generator: www.plainenglish.co.uk/examples/gobbledygook-generator.html

your report must be professional and recognisable as being from your organisation.

On one level, report writing can be exercise in branding – a marketing tool to promote your organisation, get a message across and circulate good news reports. Often, signs and symbols are used to project an image. Many organisations have a logo that has made careful use of colour and symbols. The quality of the paper, choice of typeface, use of graphs and charts and application of up-to-date technology are all representative of an organisation's culture. Make sure that the presentation is appropriate to the sector as well as the organisation: an overly glossy look can give out the wrong signal too.

Many funding reports are required to be in the receivers' styles. In addition, in-house reports often have a prescribed format. Most people can tell a *Sun* headline from a *Telegraph* headline. We use this selection process when we chose what to read.

If you are writing in a consistent house style you are displaying to the reader the image you wish them to perceive. These signs can be imperceptible but can project hidden associations that are unfortunate: one example is of an accountancy firm that insisted on addressing its clients as 'Esquire' when 'Mr' had long been the normal title used. Somehow the underlying message seemed to be: 'If you are out of date with your language, are you out of date with the tax laws, and can I trust your service?'

If your report uses Plain English, avoids gobbledygook and follows the style of your organization, you are halfway towards creating a document that will be accessible, appropriate and that people will want to read.

Chapter 5

The writing process

Writing goes through a number of stages. Keeping an overview of these is essential, as is checking all the information as you proceed.

Writing stages

The order of writing and reviewing is important. Here is one typical sequence of events:

1. Pre-writing
2. First draft and review (new ideas)
3. Second draft: and review (amendments)
4. Presentation
5. Editing
6. Circulation for comments
7. Final review
8. Proofreading

Pre-writing

Take an overview of your report before you begin to draft it. How to do this has been covered in chapters 2 and 3. Here are a couple of reminders.

Targeting: purpose and audience (chapter 2). Remember that you are writing for your readers, and not for yourself.

Planning (chapter 3). Be clear at this stage that any recommendations you will make are practicable, and offer ideas on how to follow them through.

First draft

Write your first draft without stopping to edit too much (see Editing, p. 27). This stage is about getting down the main body of the work and the appendices on to paper. Then leave your first draft for a day or two. This allows time for rethinking and for any new ideas to surface. Often, your subconscious will throw up ideas during this time.

Second draft

Once you have added in your further ideas you can move on to the conclusions, recommendations, introduction and summary of the report. (These are not usually written until after the main body and appendices have been completed, reviewed and, if necessary, redrafted.)

Leaving these until the second draft means that the conclusions and recommendations will be clearer, as you have unpacked your information during the writing of the main body. It also means that the introduction and summary will be precise and accurate.

Presentation

Presentation is everything! Instant attraction is required if you wish to encourage your reader to pick up the report and *want* to read it – so make your report look good. Choose an attractive cover. Perhaps use your organisation's logo colour. You may have to write in the prescribed house style of your organisation.

> **Top tip**
>
> Don't add page numbers to cross references until you make your final text changes. This avoids problems caused by text reflow during editing. Mark them distinctively with 'page 00', for example, so they are easy to search and replace.
>
> **John Martin, Publisher, DSC**

- Use visual clues: *italics*, underline and **bold**; but not inconsistently or all at once.
- Have a contents page or index for large reports and section the work well.
- Use cross-referencing, headings and subheadings with consistency.
- Check the 'white space' – cramped writing can signify a cramped mind. Remember that all spacing is important when providing an aesthetic piece of work.
- Use colour, pictures, graphs and diagrams: anything that can lead the reader on visually is of paramount importance.

If you make the report easy to read, the reader will want to read it.

Editing

Some people like to edit as they write, others need to let their creativity flow and then they edit at this stage in the process. Neither approach is incorrect, but both need time and, even if you edit as you go, it is advisable to have another look through at this stage.

It is difficult to write and edit at the same time. Writing is creative, exciting and experimental. Ideas flow, albeit not necessarily in the right order. Editing is a critical process that challenges your thinking and ensures that ideas are developed properly and in context. Holding the two things together can be tough.

The following table looks at the dangers of editing as you write and of editing after you have written your material.

> **Where next?**
> Go to Grammar Girl™ for some no-nonsense grammar tips: grammar.quickanddirtytips.com
> (This is an American website but it notes UK and US differences.)

Dangers of editing as you write:	Dangers of editing after you have written most of your material:
Over-editing can become a major problem. Instead of producing good ideas, the brain locks onto the words and the patterns that they form. The writer is stagnant and fossilises the concepts. Over-editing can change the original notions into something completely different, perhaps causing rewriting of other sections. This can mean that the whole report becomes a different 'animal' than was intended – often with more work attached to it than was ever needed or expected. Editing as you go stops the flow.	By starting at the beginning you may ramble on to a conclusion, convincing yourself of your own arguments. There may be a tendency to be jumbled in your thinking. You may lose pathways in the process which are harder to find at the end. Ideas can stack up very quickly but overlap or repeat themselves.

The compromise is to gather ideas, then collate them so far and then edit. Add some more material, then edit again. Most people like to edit a number of times as they write, then again at the end.

You can make your own editing checklist for each report along these lines.

Checklist

The purpose

- ❏ Have your clarified your purpose?
- ❏ Have you identified your readers' needs/ characteristics?
- ❏ Have you remembered these when considering the items below?

Information

- ❏ Have you included the main points?
- ❏ Are your points supported by evidence?
- ❏ Is the information relevant to the purpose?

Accuracy

- ❏ Are there spelling mistakes?
- ❏ Do the figures add up?
- ❏ Are the references correct, in the text and at the end?
- ❏ Are all sources of information listed in the References section?
- ❏ Are abbreviations consistent?

Images

- ❏ Are images clear?

Format

- ❏ What is the balance between sections?
- ❏ Do the most important items have the most space?
- ❏ Is the report easy to follow?
- ❏ Is it easy to find information in the report?
- ❏ Are headings and numbering clear?
- ❏ Are the arguments followed through?
- ❏ Is it logical and easy to follow?

Language

- ❏ Is it clear, direct and easy to read?
- ❏ Will the readers understand it?
- ❏ Will its tone help you achieve the purpose?
- ❏ Can unnecessary words or phrases be deleted?
- ❏ Are the grammar and punctuation correct?
- ❏ Is there any repetition?

Presentation

- ❏ Is the layout appealing?
- ❏ Does it highlight important points?

Circulation for comments

If possible, circulate drafts of your report to interested parties, asking for comments on readability, suitability or contents. You can send it out at an earlier draft

> **Where next?**
>
> If your report is long you may find your editorial decisions can be complex. Useful books on editing include: *Copy-Editing: The Cambridge Handbook for Editors, Authors and Publishers*, J Butcher, Cambridge University Press 2009 and *New Hart's Rules: The Handbook of Style for Writers and Editors* (Reference), R M Ritter, Oxford University Press, 2005.

stage, or closer to the end of the process, depending on the comments that you hope or expect to receive.

For example, if the report was commissioned, you should send out earlier drafts to ensure that you don't receive suggestions for substantial fundamental changes at the end of the process.

Allow enough time for this part of the process at whichever stage you decide to circulate the report, and give your interested parties deadlines. It can be time-consuming to get people to respond to you, and you will probably have to chase them up.

> **Top tip**
>
> Circulating a report for comments can often gain commitment to the report before its final issue.
>
> **Ben Wittenberg, Director of Publishing, Policy and Research, DSC**

Final review

Report writers often have little time to allow for this phase. However, there is always space to ask yourself a few simple questions.

Checklist

- ❏ Have you made correct connections? Ambiguities become obvious at this stage.
- ❏ Does your writing flow? Disjointed arguments or lack of signposting should become clear now.
- ❏ Can you justify your ideas? A lack of research will become evident otherwise.
- ❏ How will you be perceived? Any biases in your work will show – make sure that they are the ones that you wish to project.
- ❏ Would you be willing to give this message to your reader face-to-face? If you would not be willing to say it, do not write it.
- ❏ Have you imposed an unintended memory (see below) in your report?

Imposed memory

Try this exercise. Read the following passage quite quickly, then cover the text and answer the questions.

The checkout assistant had just shut down the till and put a closed sign across the aisle when a masked person appeared and ordered the assistant to hand over all the money in the till. The owner opened the till. The money was taken out and the masked person ran away. The assistant phoned the police.

Questions

1 What gender was the masked person?
2 Did the person demand money from the store owner?
3 Did the assistant hand over the money?

Answers

1 It is not mentioned. (Although we are not told the gender of the masked person, often we prescribe one.)
2 Yes. (Were you clear that the assistant was ordered to hand over the money? Details can get crossed in the memory's pictures.)
3 It is not made clear. (The passive phrase 'the money was taken out' leaves us unsure who handed over the money.)

When we write we can impose memories on our readers, so we need to be sure that they are the correct ones.

Find someone that you trust (and who is unfamiliar with the report) who can read your text to make sure that no unintended connections have been made, and that the writing is clear and unambiguous. This can be the same person that you ask to proofread the report.

Proofreading

Once your document is in its (very near) final form – as it would be were it to be distributed – it is ready to be proofread.

As the writer of your report, you should never do the proofreading yourself: you are far too involved to be able to notice any little errors that will remain, and remain they always do. Choose the most appropriate person in your organisation (there is usually at least one person who is known for being good at this sort of thing), and ask them in advance whether they could put aside some time to proofread the report. Given enough notice and the right approach, most people are willing to do this.

Once the final changes following the proofread have been taken in, your report is ready to be distributed.

Rewards

When you have completed a report, you deserve a reward. The process of report writing is challenging, but should be interesting and fulfilling. Rewards can be self-awarded or, better still, come from the report's commissioning agent or the readers.

Wherever it comes from, enjoy your reward. It can help to make your next report writing something to look forward to!

Continuous improvement

Report writing is something you will get better at, the more you do it. So don't forget, as part of the learning cycle, to request constructive feedback from your readers.

Where next?

Writing for Work, Moi Ali, DSC, 2009:
www.dsc.org.uk/Publications/SpeedReadSeries